T0119066

ALPHABET

Words by Robin Feiner

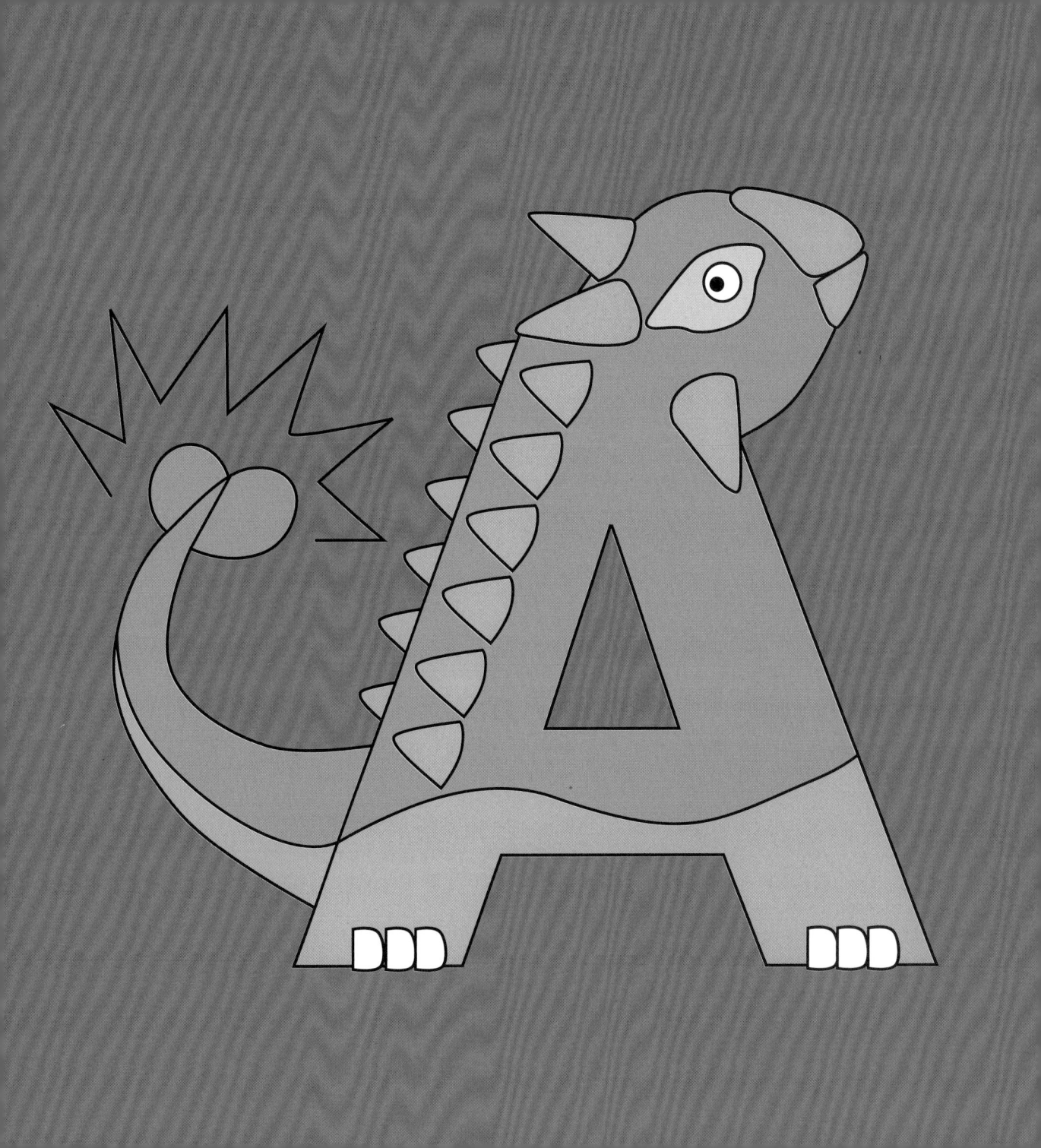

Aa

A is for Ankylosaurus.
[an-key-low-sawr-us]
Similar to a crocodile or armadillo, the Ankylosaurus had huge plates of bone built into its skin to protect it against attackers. It also used its long, strong tail as a club! Now that's some legendary body armor!

B is for Brontosaurus.
[bron-tah-sawr-us]
With its long neck and even longer tail, the Brontosaurus was one of the largest creatures to ever walk the Earth. By the time it was 10 years old, it had already reached full size – about 75 feet tall!

Cc

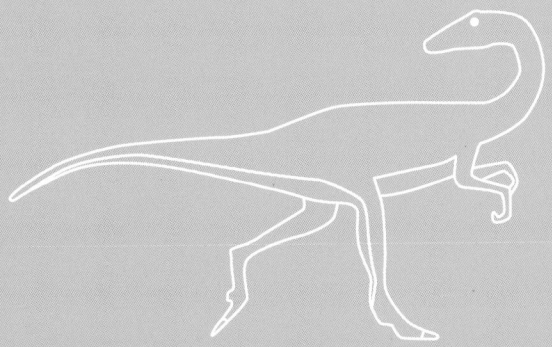

C is for Coelophysis.
[seel-oh-fie-sis]
It may have been small, but this two-legged hunter was fast! It also had excellent vision thanks to its big forward-facing eyes. Coelophysis lived in the Triassic period, and may have traveled in packs.

Dd

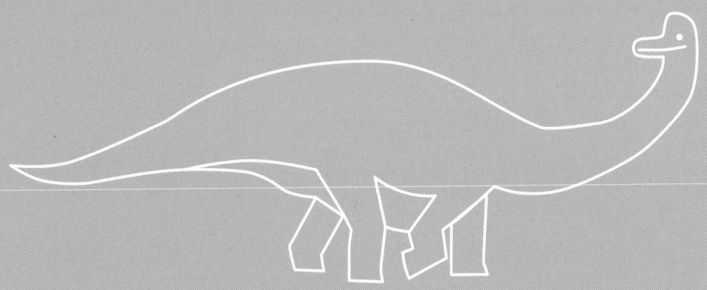

D is for Diplodocus.
[di-plo-duh-kuhs]
If you've ever been to a dinosaur museum, chances are you've seen the large skeleton belonging to the Diplodocus on display. This plant-eater with strong legs has also been featured in many popular movies and cartoons.

Ee

is for iniosaurus.
[eye-knee-o-sawr-us]
With its long snout horn and neck frills, it's easy to see why scientists gave it a name meaning 'buffalo lizard!' Einiosaurus was a plant-eating dinosaur that most likely lived in herds with its relatives.

F is for Fukuisaurus.
[foo-koo-eye-sawr-us]
Believed to only be about 6 feet tall, the Fukuisaurus was pretty small for a dinosaur! So far, scientists have found only one set of fossil remains (in Japan) of this rare dinosaur that lived around 129 million years ago.

Gg

G is for Gallimimus.
[gal-ih-my-muss]
This two-legged dinosaur from the Cretaceous period was fast and agile – much like an ostrich, but with a tail! Gallimimus also had a bird-like beak, which was shaped like a shovel so it could easily scoop up food.

H is for Hylaeosaurus.
[hi-lay-ah-sawr-us]
One of the first dinosaurs to be discovered, Hylaeosaurus may not have been big, but it was tough – with a big bony plate around its hips, and rows of horns all down its back and shoulders.

I is for Iguanodon.
[ig-wah-na-don]
The Iguanodon had unique thumbs with spikes on them to protect it and help it gather food. But when scientists first discovered this legendary plant-eater in 1822, they thought the thumb spike was its nose!

Jj

J is for Jobaria.
[joe-bare-ee-ah]
This West African giant was one of the most complete long-necked dinosaur skeletons ever discovered. Its flexible neck meant it could stand up on its back legs to reach food or fight off attackers.

K is for Kentrosaurus.
[ken-tro-sawr-us]
Originating from the Jurassic period, this slow-walking dinosaur's name means 'spiky lizard,' and that's exactly what it looked like – with different types of spikes all the way from its back down to its tail!

L is for Lambeosaurus.
[lam-bee-o-sawr-us]
Named after Lawrence Lambe, a Canadian fossil hunter, Lambeosaurus was the first duck-billed dinosaur found in North America. It had a hollow, bony crest on its head, pebbly skin and over 1,000 teeth!

Mm

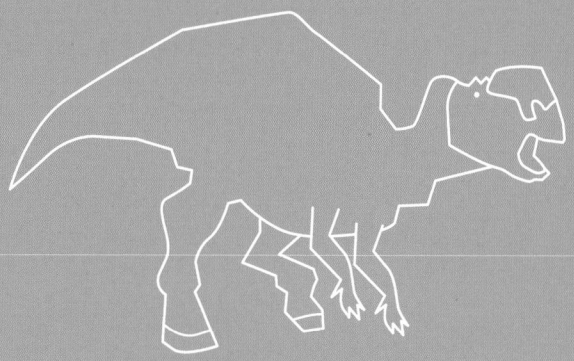

M is for Muttaburrasaurus. [mew-tah-burr-ah-sawr-us] What sets this Australian dinosaur apart is its rounded snout with a bump on the top. Scientists believe this bump was hollow, which could have made Muttaburrasaurus' voice louder and sense of smell stronger.

Nn

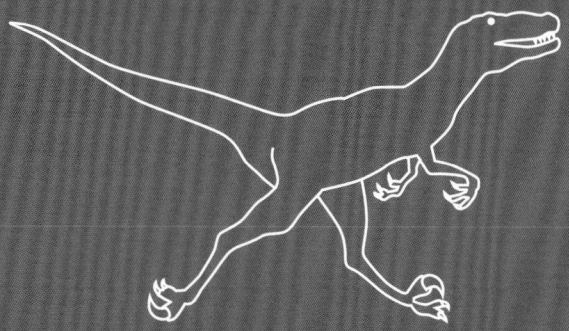

N is for Noasaurus.
[no-ah-sawr-us]
Although it only grew to be about 3 feet tall and 7 feet long, this small meat-eater was still an expert hunter, using its claws skillfully. Noasaurus lived in South America, with scientists finding fossils in northwest Argentina.

O is for Oviraptor.
[oh-vih-rap-tor]
With its parrot-like head, three-fingered clawed hands and powerful jaw, Oviraptor was quite a unique dinosaur! Found sitting on a nest, scientists gave it a name meaning 'egg thief' – but later discovered it was protecting, not stealing, the eggs!

Pp

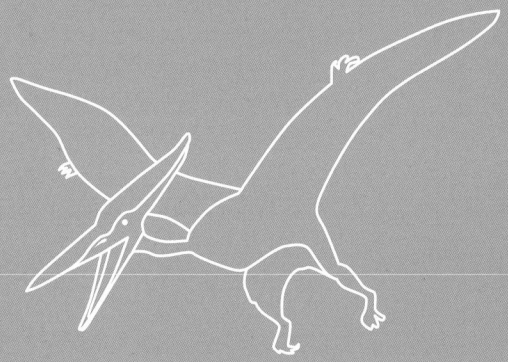

P is for Pterodactyl.
[tare-oh-dack-til]
This creature is often called a dinosaur but it's actually a type of 'pterosaur,' which is a flying reptile. With its pointy beak and leathery wings, the Pterodactyl soared across the skies during the Jurassic period.

Qq

Q is for Quetzalcoatlus.
[ket-sal-koh-at-lus]
Named after the Aztec
feathered god 'Quetzalcoatl,'
this flying reptile (or pterosaur) used
its large brain and big eyes to spot
its prey from the sky then glided
toward the water and
swooped it up!

Rr

R is for Rugops.
[roo-gops]
Much about this medium-sized meat-eater is still a mystery, but a skull found in the year 2000 led scientists to believe that the Rugops may have used special facial features to make itself seem bigger and scarier than it actually was!

S is for Stegosaurus.
[steg-ah-sawr-us]
You probably know what it looks like from a movie or cartoon, but did you know that the Stegosaurus is the State Dinosaur for Colorado? That's because Colorado is where the first Stegosaurus fossil was found!

ROAR

T is for **T**yrannosaurus rex.
[tie-ran-ah-sawr-us-rex]
T. rex was one of the fiercest meat-eaters that ever lived. Around 40 feet long with the most powerful head and biggest teeth of all the dinosaurs, the only creature it had to fear was another T. rex! Legendary!

Uu

U is for Udanoceratops.
[u-dan-oh-ser-ah-tops]
First discovered in the Udan-Sayr area in Mongolia, Udanoceratops was a horn-faced plant-eater that used its beak-like mouth to clip off parts of plants and ferns. It also had small neck frills and a solid tail.

Vv

V is for Velociraptor.
[vell-oss-ee-rap-tor]
If you've ever watched 'Jurassic Park,' you would've seen that the Velociraptor was fierce, smart and fast. One of the most legendary fossils ever found was of this hunter using its powerful foot claw to attack a Protoceratops!

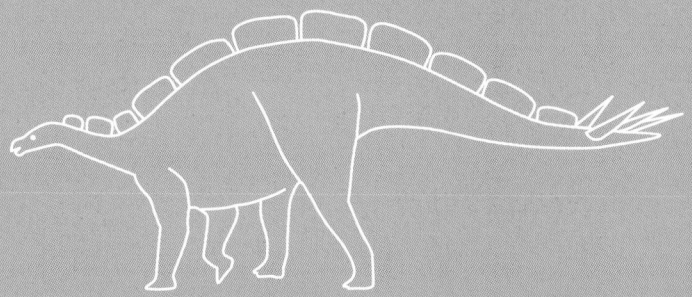

W is for Wuerhosaurus.
[woo-er-huh-sawr-us]
Similar to the Stegosaurus, this dinosaur had two rows of long, bony plates from its neck all the way down to its back and tail. It also ate plants that grew low to the ground.

Xx

X is for Xenoceratops.
[zee-no-ser-ah-tops]
With a giant spiked frill and horns shaped like a spear, 'alien horned-face' was an earlier cousin of the Triceratops. It lived around 78 million years ago and was only discovered in the year 2012!

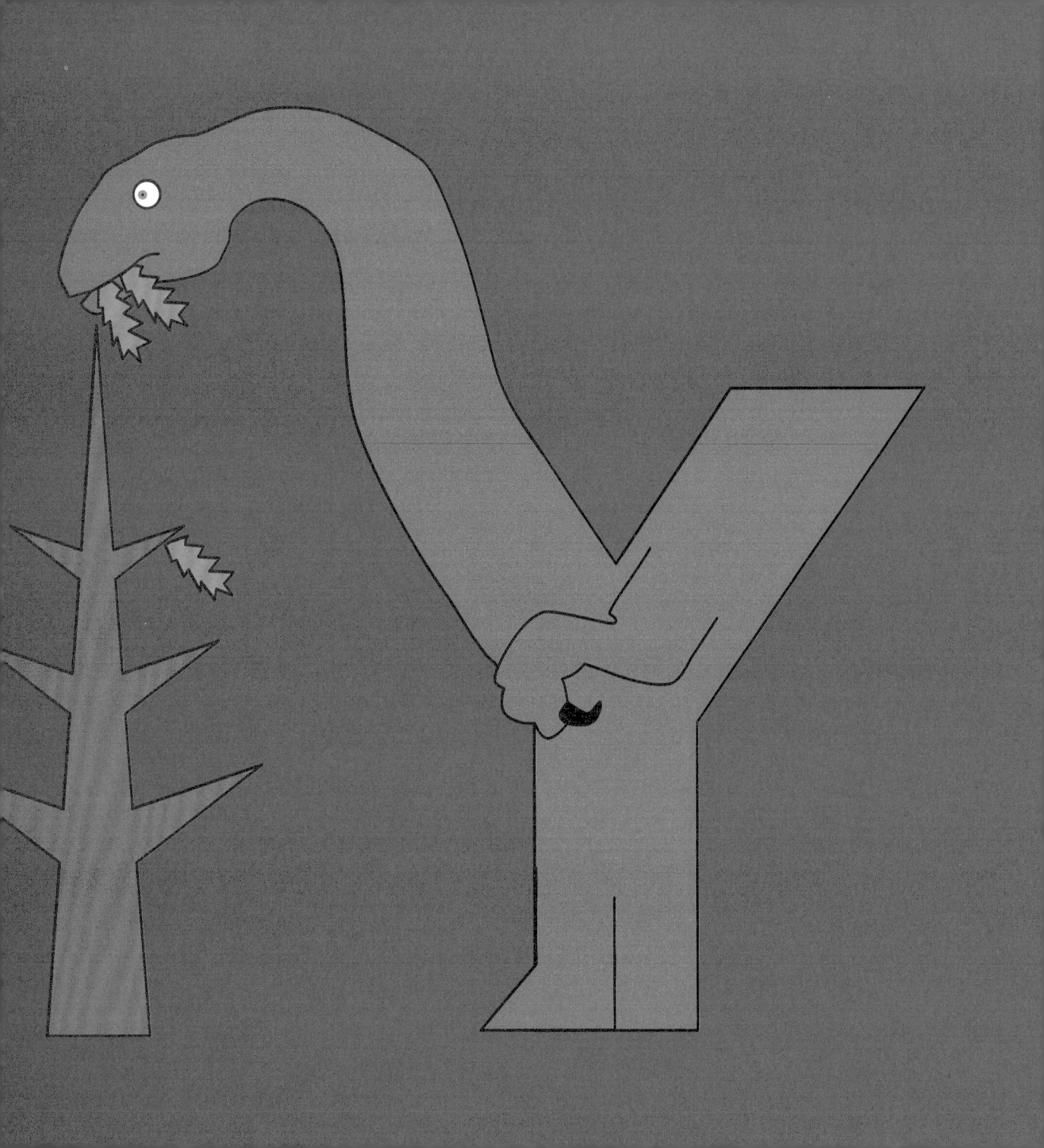

Yy

Y is for Yunnanosaurus.
[you-nan-oh-sawr-us]
Over 20 specimens have been found belonging to Yunnanosaurus, which lived in Asia around 195 million years ago. It had spoon-shaped teeth that rubbed against each other while it ate as a way of sharpening themselves!

Zz

Z is for Zuniceratops.
[zoo-nee-ser-ah-tops]
Zuniceratops may have been around 90 million years old, but it was discovered by an 8-year-old boy out on a dig with his father! It just goes to show, you're never too young to be a paleontologist!